WILLIAM STAFFORD

Smoke's Way

POEMS FROM LIMITED EDITIONS 1968-1981

GRAYWOLF PRESS

PORT TOWNSEND, WASHINGTON

Poems included in this volume were selected from fourteen limited edition books, chapbooks and pamphlets. We are grateful to the editors and publishers of the following presses (people who are often also illustrators, bookbinders, printers . . .), whose care for literature and the making of books is an example for all publishers.

Walter and Mary Hamady, Perishable Press Limited, publishers of *Eleven Untitled Poems* (1968), *Weather* (1969), *That Other Alone* (1973) and *Tuft by Puff* (1978).

Duane Schneider, whose Duane Schneider Press published *Temporary Facts* (1970); and whose Croissant & Company published *All About Light* (1978).

Robert Sward, Soft Press, Canada, who issued *In the Clock of Reason* (1973).

William Fox, West Coast Poetry Review Press, publisher of *Going Places* (1975).

Karen and John Sollid, Spring Rain Press, publisher of *North by West* (1975).

Keith Browning, Confluence Press, publisher of *Braided Apart* (1976).

Elizabeth Coberly, Night Heron Press, publisher of *The Design on the Oriole* (1977).

Douglas and Carol Woolf, Nadja Press, publishers of *The Quiet of the Land* (1979).

Tree Swenson and Sam Hamill, Copper Canyon Press, publishers of *Sometimes Like a Legend* (1981).

ISBN 0-915308-40-1
ISBN 0-915308-41-X (paperback)
Library of Congress #83-80525

First Printing, 1983
9 8 7 6 5 4 3 2

Publication of this volume is made possible in part by a grant from the National Endowment for the Arts, Washington, D.C.

Published by Graywolf Press, Post Office Box 142, Port Townsend, Washington 98368.

CONTENTS

I   IN SOMEBODY'S BIG SHELL OF THE SKY:
STARTING FROM HOME IN THE 1940's AND 1950's

Storm Warning, 3

Shells, 4

Inland Murmur, 5

Attenuate, 6

Discovery, 7

Temporary Facts, 8

Outreach, 9

Not Policy, But Love, 10

No One Who Trusts, 11

The Last Time, 12

Toad, 13

At the Cabin, 14

Proportioning, 15

The Design on the Oriole, 16

II   IDENTITY: WANDERINGS IN THE 1960's

A Letter Not Even to Deliver, 19

Before Anyone Died, 20

Beaver People, 21

A Walk with My Father When I Was Eight, 22

R_x Creative Writing: Identity, 23

The Girl Who Died, Who Lived, 24

Even Now, 25

The Day I Got the Good Idea, 26

It Rode with Us, 27

Tourist Country, 28

Maybe Alone on My Bike, 29

Light, and My Sudden Face, 30

On Her Slate at School, 31

A Farewell Picture, 32

Time Capsule, 33

Fort Rock, 34

In the Cold, 35

At Missoula, 36

Survival, 37

Brother, 38

Snapshot, 39

Storm at the Coast, 40

Viewing the Coast, 41

Just to Let You Know, 42

The Stranger, 43

The Coyote in the Zoo, 44

Remembering a First-Grade Music Teacher, 45

After Spring and Summer, 46

Outside of Town, 47

In Our State No One Ever, 48

When We Got to Chitina, 49

That Autumn Instant, 50

The Indian Cave Jerry Ramsey Found, 51

North of Liberal, 52

The Summer Game, 53

The Little Room, 54

III ANIMALS FULL OF LIGHT: POEMS 1970-1972

Kinship, 57

At the Apostle Islands, 58

Aquarium at Seaside, 59

Ferns, 60

A Quiet Day at the Beach, 61

Mr. Fear, 62

Those Leaves, 63

Remnants of a Poem, Obscure Parts Burned Away
    in a Freak Accident at the Office of
    the *Westigan Review*, 64

Saturday Nights, 65

Rambling On, 66

Early Morning, 67

Some Lights, 68

Terms of Surrender, 69

At Archbishop Lamy's Church in Santa Fe, 70

At the Edge of Town, 71

Where We Live, 72

A Glimpse by the Path, 73

Canadian, 74

The Way It Will Be, 75

A Church Keeps On, 76

Then, 77

Any Journey, 78

The Conditions, 79

It's Like Wyoming, 80

Tonight, 81

Beginning the Day, 82

Meditation, 83

IV FINDING SMOKE'S WAY: POEMS 1973-1977

Our Life, 87

West of Here, 88

The Saint of Thought, 89

A Gift for Kit, 90

Things About the Sun, 91

Slants of Rain, 92

Many Things Are Hidden by the Light, 93

Cave Painting, 94

By the Deschutes Shore, 95

At an Interval in Talk, 96

Stillness Is the Right Wave, 97

Across Nebraska, 98

Gutters of Jackson: Cache Street North, 99

For a Marker, 100

Happy in Sunlight, 101

Another Twilight, 102

Charged by Moonlight, 103

Assurance, 104

The Way I Do It, 105

Looking for You, 106

Smoke, 107

An Alphabetical List of Titles, 109

Smoke's Way

FROM SMALL PRESS COLLECTIONS, MOST OF WHICH
ARE NOW OUT OF PRINT, THIS BOOK SELECTS POEMS
NOT ELSEWHERE GATHERED IN BOOK FORM. THE
SEQUENCE IS BY DATE OF COMPOSITION, RANGING
FROM 1947 TO 1977.

I

IN SOMEBODY'S BIG SHELL OF THE SKY:
STARTING FROM HOME IN THE 1940's AND 1950's

STORM WARNING

Something not the wind shakes along far
like a sky truck in low gear
over Oregon. Like the shore wind baying
               along through fir
but not now the wind, no, not really so,
it is a new weight and force
that begins to blow.

This winter they'll still call it wind and let it explore;
and when they talk it over next summer
               there by the shore,
along through the scrub and salal
               the new something will range.
In a hurry, late, it won't wait for the air.

In the fall again they'll remember,
               each of them, back to now.
They'll no longer call it wind, they'll want it all changed.
They'll want it all different then,
               but they won't know how.

SHELLS

When they turn the dial to "know"
there on the beach or the grass
they speak low
and then stop to hear,
wanting the message—
like holding a shell to the ear.

And the shell to each one
returns the life sound,
the rustle of breath
and the live surge.
Eyes grow round
and each hears his own words.

And the grass only asks
its question again,
as far and as true as the roots can go,
and as long and straight and as high
as the rain blows
in the shell of the sky,

In somebody's big shell of the sky.

INLAND MURMUR

In the Cimarron Hills
on the sod no plowshare knew
pigeons tumbled through the air
and on the grassblades there
the rain fell in the dark
and the wind blew.

On the Cimarron Rock
the crooked water broke
a splash and then a swirl
from arid gorges gritted full
far in the softest curve
of the Cimarron Hills.

On the swell of earth
or in the swirling flood, I knew
tumbling clear the pigeon feel
and the rain touch as the wind blew
over the curve the world was of
in the Cimarron Hills.

ATTENUATE

Some time, following out a sound,
the way to come back will disappear,
and into new country a long fine ear
will reach, to hear those places beyond
the just whispering of things. In Heaven
gifts are made real by not being given.

DISCOVERY

Plowing the nest of the lark
we breasted a sudden wave—
all the furrows in all the farms
and all the birds disturbed.

There gleamed from where we came
one long continuous line—
fields where men had walked,
on many a nest of song.

TEMPORARY FACTS

That look you had, Agnes, was a temporary fact.
Probably by now Time has it back.
From spiral nebulae I call it here now.

Through the trance of high school you pass along
                    the hall.
Lockers clang the hours; you pass windows.
A Christmas candle shines on your hair.

On spellbound evenings you call your brother home,
coming toward the streetlight through shadows
                    of the elm.
Shadows touch your mouth when you say a name.

All of these things were temporary facts.
Only for an instant Time gives them back.
In spiral nebulae a shadow goes on.

OUTREACH

In the barefoot dark without a cry
waiting for ones that never will return,
fog speaking back to the foghorn, dawn
fading, our boat at the foot of morning—
I know so much of darkness that it drowns.
There will be audit of this careless river,
many a stone fire-kissed in its bed of mud
or shrilled to exist with an instant leap
then vaporing gone, and the loss will curl:
in the barefoot dark I face that kind of world.
But through it runs a course, one deeper stream
that could be mine, a way even murderers learn
swung down goodby with their caught hands.
From hate, from less than hate, they find
a way in the dark where the farthest water extends.
We feel a net come silvering through the land.

NOT POLICY, BUT LOVE

Regarding river lights
(my life has been variously lived)
was just a quiet thing
I sometimes did.

Those river lights have shone
in a way to save our home,
for beyond our jealous walls
were lights, or dawn—

Calm lights, not policy
but love: those river lights
were love without intent
lost in the night.

Through dark their pearlness poured
far over the glistening tide.
I watched those river lights
with long regard.

NO ONE WHO TRUSTS

No one who trusts words can learn
things from stone.
We have lost forever
the purposes around us.

Climbing a mountain we lay
an ear against pine,
but the roots turn away from air
for stiller friends.

In walls and paving tomorrow,
whatever is dumb
may lift the cry of patience
earth teaches her children.

And those who hear such voices
then on the shared air
may turn from words and listen
toward the stone.

THE LAST TIME

They headed toward the Platte, a lawn like Texas:
their chances every night were fair
when they let the campfires die and heard the miles
                    lie down.
Above their need the quartering stars
began to hunt. Fall was in the air.

One night their blanket faces caught excitement:
snow across dark passes. Campfires ate
the promise wood. By dawn, evangelist,
the mountains reared—a map of winter,
a clear report: all peaks had surrendered.

By authority of space and silence General Miles
struck through deer trail amazement in pursuit
till scouts read snow by Cheyenne blood and heard
upwind the dying strike their wintry song
in the scenery of their fathers, their centuries' end.

TOAD

Hop, hope. Hop again.
Hunch, lunch. Hunch on then.
Streetlight starer,
waistcoat wearer,
every night—remember?

Corner blinker, eyes that come on,
hometown calm one—
toward stars you stared,
a look moths rode.
Stars are still there,

Summer slummer,
soft night learner,
kind of a drain for sound,
reminding of canyons in the ocean
and of how birds dream their songs,

But gone from your side, vortex for noise,
I have not found, blinker of worlds,
any dreamer who stood
so slouch in the mud
as you, at the corner each night.

AT THE CABIN

Across the snowed-in roof
winter drags a foot
like a timid person
interrupting us—

For I am thinking of you.
Clear from the top window
west from this house
the day bends on, downward;

And through that top window
hills dodge everywhere,
all the hills freezing
in one cold fire.

It's a wild target
winter has made:
this cabin in the center
of a silence around your name.

PROPORTIONING

At any proud hour the flame
God owes may reach my name: at any hour.

In every storm the warmth of wool
may hide last things. I know.

All times by grace pour hours
across the glance we take. We pause,

Hearing the level wind. We note:
animals crowd this ark this night.

Then we go on.

THE DESIGN ON THE ORIOLE

Dragon blood, they say—little emblems
of orange with wings, in-and-out horsehair bills,
late tails, eager heads unwinding a code,
a message from someone.
Maybe right here we are being told.

"I try," the pattern says;
"I burn cameo feather designs
around a whole star"—some such frantic message
in the simple trees,
the world's curious crescendo shout reaching us.

The design seems far, and even splinters a little,
so faint we can't reach it,
can't understand.
And artists have died receiving these many
secret little punches through the hands.

II

IDENTITY: WANDERINGS IN THE 1960's

A LETTER NOT EVEN TO DELIVER

The world often has a quiet look.
I go down in the orchard quietly
to work every day, because trees keep
trouble away and a grove makes quiet work.

But a jagged glimpse can come—say, when a bird sings
down a row, or over toward a hill. I bow
to near views, and listen close, for this one day:
splendor is not for daily things,

And a bowed back is a disguise. I remember you, fair.
If you visit me, come some quiet way.
There might be an instant; the light might flame—
be quiet then. We are not to try far.

Only the brownest birds that come here belong here.

BEFORE ANYONE DIED

West of home where we lay talking quietly
—a place not there any more—
we knew the rain coming near a thousand ways
and without color the hills very softly appearing
one by one and then becoming night, its wall,
and like up a well stars being steady after the rain.

We'd not known that place before, west of home.
But like the tribe whose talk turned real
we said we'd value everything from where
we were, before anyone died, like this:
"Every ritual time they breathe,
you hold a million dollars in your hand."

BEAVER PEOPLE

Beaver people are trying to figure out the good water.
All winter they feel a dark deep touch
around their house. "Somewhere," one says, "there is
the good water." But another one, drowsing with a paw
over the edge of the bunk, just says,
"But how could it be different, very much?"

Around them sweep currents from up-country—
whatever happened there: leaves, dirt, a spring
that flowed a slow promise every day last summer.
To live—real—in their house is to belong to all that,
yielding to it a face of many-muscled confession: where
you have been—a face that never avoided anything.

Beaver people swirl that scenario for us; trail
before our faces too a world streaming
ready for our kind of knowing, a river in thought-color.
They declare the Renaissance in any patch of alders.
While we drowse, a paw flips to all of us drowned here
in our own pageant, under this ice, dreaming.

A WALK WITH MY FATHER WHEN I WAS EIGHT

Here is a space for the way the day started:
(_____).
Here is a word for the sun: (_____).
I can't fill these blanks for sure any more:
that day we were both young.

He showed me the creek I thought people dug—
a wild thing, we found, wandering;
we saw clenched lovers—"two spooners," he said:—
so calm he tamed even that wind.

By rich people's farms (they owned the world
and up into hills that held
a place in the sky) we sang for their cows,
and belonged there, tramping their fields.

In town by dusk we owned such a day
that other days lined out through school
and on out: I could find them and live every one,
after that walk through the fields.

R_x CREATIVE WRITING: IDENTITY

You take this pill, a new world
springs out of whatever sea
most drowned the old one,
arrives like light.

Then that bone light belongs
inside of things. You touch
or hear so much *yourself*
there is no dark,

Nothing left but what Aquinas
counted: he—touched, luminous—
bowed over sacred worlds, each one
conceived, then really there—

Not just hard things: down on
a duck as real as steel.
You know so sure there burns
a central vividness.

It tells you;
all you do is tell about it.

THE GIRL WHO DIED, WHO LIVED

Last night an old sound came by chance;
dust regained its honest place
the way it stopped when years ago
that little girl who died, who lived
across our street, was lying in the rain
we played in till the church bell rang.

Back then we thought the minutes came
one at a time; but in the sound
that came by chance all minutes leaped
at once and bore me down, remembering.
I stood a stranger chance had struck
or bells had caught; I leaned on dust,

Heard the storm bring the neighborhood
onto our porch that afternoon,
gathered for help, all talking at once,
trying to regain our quiet place
before the girl who lived had died.
Fingers in the rain still identify her face.

EVEN NOW

Wherever I go such winter shakes our town
that I look at the ground and feel the storm
               that shudders to get in.
Wherever I go, it's night there; weather
buffets at the stores while people listen—
listen: furious echoes batter the roof
               and rattle the tin.

Wherever I go the whole world's air
caught in a river rushes the door to bend and pound
hinges that strain and whine out a myth:
"Here's where it all could start again;
again, wanderer—
               now! Turn round!"

Wherever I go, whoever I become,
that Christmas weather wheels through streets
               and the alleys behind,
and—remote and secure though I thought
               to have been—
for thousands of nights a tin sign has flapped,
flapped a message I can't quite read,
               caught in such wind.

THE DAY I GOT THE GOOD IDEA

Had the right amount of rain, wind pushing it,
air cold as it should be, and a mountain
shaped for this kind of winter; all that could
happen caught there in refraction: tachistoscope—
the whole state in photographs by drops of rain.

I wandered with a dog too fierce to neglect
its guard of what ought to be: all that fair land,
protected by our footsteps, loomed;
and we bore what he smelled, though he confessed
fast with his tail all our walk made him understand.

So—it was a window day, a contact lens,
the fine-print world declaring the verb "to be,"
on stone the Constitution engraved everywhere
                    all the time,
and myself halted, suddenly knowing, smiling, wise—
like standing barefoot on the picture on a dime.

IT RODE WITH US

All things had their place. Even the wind
had a steady song, and any bullets,
even, that came would have right arcs
or ricochet, "Belong!"

Whatever fell traced Newton's hand, or God's,
all grace and speed; and what appeared
no matter where we looked was right
and had found our need.

All was determined so well that justice
felt sweet in the ear, rode home with us
and called wherever my father drove,
"Here, here, here."

TOURIST COUNTRY

Shadows, like Navahoes, wear velvet
like the Navahoes, and they too have silver,
carry a blanket over a shoulder,
and guard gold corn in its earth hogan.

Light here always demands—where?
when it comes. Day turns it on
and it will stay, hold pictures against the wall;
it props cliffs above churches all over Mexico.

Glances go feathery and fringed, use
little of the available light; stares are rationed
among Indians, can measure how far
you are from, and polish your shoes.

Stones here meet the sun abrupt,
one edge at a time. What can yearn outward
more than these big rocks? Each one
cools fast in the dark and re-learns at night

—Oh so sincerely—its local part.

MAYBE ALONE ON MY BIKE

I listen, and the mountain lakes
hear snowflakes come on those winter wings
only the owls are awake to see,
their radar gaze and furred ears
alert. In that stillness a meaning shakes;

And I have thought (maybe alone
on my bike, quaintly on a cold
evening pedaling home) think!—
the splendor of our life, its current unknown
as those mountains, the scene no one sees.

Oh citizens of our great amnesty:
we might have died. We live. Marvels
coast by, great veers and swoops of air
so bright the lamps waver in tears,
and I hear in the chain a chuckle I like to hear.

LIGHT, AND MY SUDDEN FACE

I am the man whose heart for
four days lost in a cave
beat when the water dripped:
I was found, and the water stopped,
never to start again.
Now even the cave is lost
where the lost, in order to hear,
held the whole breath of the earth.

In the night I strike a match,
one little glory, a flame
the world surrounds, a stutter
that leaps as the light goes out
and the trail to the cave begins:
impenetrably disguised as myself
I range the whole world in the dark
to hammer on doors with my heart.

ON HER SLATE AT SCHOOL

On her slate at school my mother wrote "Winter."
When she ran home the weather erased it.
For all the pain my mother saw in the world,
over her face the snow has exploded its little flowers.

"This is the part of the year," she called to us,
"excluded from tree rings: children, remember!"
Around our house were such tall legends,
everything carved by winds and rivers.

Even today they care, the temporary winds,
the prevailing rivers; and a giant in disguise
still knocks at our chimney. For awhile, children,
the trees around us have those years in them.

A FAREWELL PICTURE

My eyes look their twinned corridor far,
focus for a while, then lose again that
year it snowed the picture of the world
and radio clocks learned war by heart all night.

My father nailed only game with his rifle.
People, no; only the game—until
that year mistakes came up his arm and
shattered our snowflake faith's integrity.

Steady as ever was, but never again
so clear, so eager to be blind—
I see again and again that great snowflake
smash on my father's face like a valentine.

TIME CAPSULE

That year the news
was a storm, a wind that
puzzled monuments. Wrecks piled up
on the Coast, and at year's end
after the party and song we sang
our old composition called "Friend,"
wrapped up the scraps for the stock;
then one by one
through perspective we took up coat
and hat and
were gone,
westward up the river
where flood-mangled cottonwoods
imitated grotesquely Governor
and President and Saint, bend by
bend, all the way home.

That year the news was
not only free, it was mandatory.
The barometer said "War."
To the west gulls came
in like tracers.

Back on the farm it was calm,
and pigs ate the greasy newspapers.

FORT ROCK

Dead grass makes an arc on the sand
as the wind veers. Wild flowers
follow the road there.
And think how long that still
stone balanced above the Indian cave,
falling toward them all the time
at their front door.

IN THE COLD

When I got out of the rocket
the little handle broke.
Now I couldn't go back.

I wanted to tell them all
but I dared not speak—
every heart would freeze;

For in any instant, one
next breath exists—one.
And if it should be displaced!

We ran that rocket on
one long explosion
steadier than the strongest hand,

But—peril of the great sky—
a flaw had found us out
and God was counting us

As we were counting Him
(for every ten of us,
that's His hands again).

And listen: the wind has come.
Finally, it always does.
It will touch everything.

AT MISSOULA

We hunted bitterroot over the patient mountain,
tasted hundreds of kinds of flowers, bruised
and smelled and nibbled stalk, root, leaves,
our need some radical, corm, blossom, or stem—
to eat flesh on the mountain, hear the thread
                              of our summer
hum past wild rose or dozing rock. And lodged
on the hillside in the wild rose thicket we found
a tiny song so subtle the air goes back
and forth to find it again, and hunting so, makes it.

The Blackfoot roamed here, looked up, faltered. Where
we found the wild roses, they found the great rock
that could roll over on them and be theirs. We tasted
that root, and all the cool mountain filled its place,
became a serene shawl, belonged at our feet
and over us, formed a new state and acted out
its one-word constitution: Patience.

SURVIVAL

Evenings, we call quail.
The desert sends those lightfoot troops
against us down the trail.

So straight they tread their path,
so small, so soft, birdshot at twenty yards
for them is death.

Or step, step toward a noose
we lightly pray them on,
and let our starved eyes choose.

Then more world than they knew—more night—
comes down. For you, survivors, for you,
I shoot in this tricky light.

BROTHER

It's cold where Bob is:
I'm glad the rich have cozy
homes, and anyone can huddle.

Out there, it's cold
and Bob has gone so far
no one in the world can touch his hand.

Such broken years as
he had, now belong
to others. I turn to them, to live.

But Bob was.
He lived.
I had a brother.

SNAPSHOT

A hand reaches over the edge of rock
at the last waterfall up Eagle Creek,
and clenches on a ledge to draw up
head, shoulders, body, and finally
muddy boots of a climber.
He turns to look out westerly
where the sun hangs just before dusk,
ready to touch millions of embraced
firs along the main ridge.

At the man's feet on the pool's edge
tatters of river foam lift and
hurry distractedly over the stone.
After a few breaths he resumes:
places a hand up the ledge, levers himself,
and disappears on up, while his tracks
fill with water, the dark, the lapsed
fringe of foam. In the big empty
night the sound of the current frills along.

STORM AT THE COAST

What moves on, moves far,
here. What holds, holds long.
But it is the wind and water will stay,
after the cliffs are gone.

VIEWING THE COAST

A tracker from Neptune
came up the sand, over the dunes,
through the grass,
and lost like millions of steps of the rain
became part of the world.

You inquire at homes, farm
after farm: no such wanderer.
But there had to be: the sand
reports how the smooth dune
accepted what came.

And after the beach, every way
you turn calls the eye
to track what comes, and offers
day with its rivers of light
that help you arrive,

At all that there is, like rain.

JUST TO LET YOU KNOW

The road from Bend, looking for a way
to serve, ignores the scenery—remember how?
I was up at your cabin, Terrell, to question
the snow: no one has cared this winter
whether you were at home. The mountains that never
heard of troubles are still wise
and alone; the junipers wander roundshouldered
on the slower hills.

Without even knowing what I
wanted to know, I have come home.
Those things we can do, we do, and you
do well. And your place is all right.
But I wanted to say:
at the edge of the road, lost, without tracks,
under the snow, unsurprised along your
walks in the silent junipers—what you
went there for, the other things—
they are still up there.

THE STRANGER

The place he wanted to tell about
lay beyond, lay far. It had
no name; it hardly differed from this,
but it was apart, and thus deserved
our thought. He spoke on.

There were bushes he wanted us
to see. And the rocks had a certain
subdued gleam when the sun came;
they were not precious, just different,
and other, and odd. . . .

A mountain was there that
you could not see from here.
A stream just smaller than ours bent
and made a park where in winter
deer and elk spelled out their trails.

He spoke on. The world had
such special and lost places in it!
He shook his head when we offered
him a rest. No, no, he would be
getting along. Those bushes—
they had little berries, like salal,
to eat, but sour, but. . . .

After he left I felt insignificant things:
leaf prints on my hands,
at my heels the tug of my shadow,
—the hollow away off there, waiting—
towns where we almost lived.

THE COYOTE IN THE ZOO

A yellow eye meets mine;
I suddenly know, too late,
the land outside belongs
to the one that looks away.

REMEMBERING A FIRST-GRADE
MUSIC TEACHER

Her non-representational near face
fixed my gaze on local dramatics—
the old skin, lines of storm and calm, eyebrows.
And there behind her glasses, in those lakes that
forgot summer, I found the numb center, then slid
away, outward, upward, outward. . . .

The service of those stern ones, the knowers,
the ones who demand a further note,
has lifelong set me toward islands,
toward fields tested by nothing but grass,
toward stones at the coast that hold amid waves.
And in church I never sing.

AFTER SPRING AND SUMMER

Sometimes a wind mentions your (cloud) face,
your (leaf) address, your (wire-strum) name;
and the whole world then turns into a telegram:
"Stop, stop, stop. Yours always," unsigned,
but addressed clear back to the cloud, leaf,
wire-strum town where that wind first came.

OUTSIDE OF TOWN

Loud sparrows hidden
in a leafy little tree:
decisions! decisions!

Hummingbird by a
tempting flower: all that work
to keep from moving!

And flowers on a
hillside: common dirt holds all
this hidden color.

Look at that summer!
And I help the world have it
all, just by breathing.

IN OUR STATE NO ONE EVER

No one ever cared
how the rain looked. It wore
capes and long hair mostly and
sandals or gym shoes. It would
lounge along, testing puddles and dead
leaves and anything else it found friendly.

No one ever found
where the rain lived. It would
come on dark days, broadshouldered
over the Coast Range, and stay
casually chattering at intervals, often
through dinner and even late at night.

I followed it once,
east into the mountains. It leaned
and with a last pat it turned away
into one of those canyons no road
has found. It likes the dark, I thought,
and has a steady friend in the west wind.

No one ever helped
the rain, though, enough—oh,
travelers and children maybe, a little.
And some of us who held Scripture in mind,
or had old things to touch,
we held out a hand.

WHEN WE GOT TO CHITINA

No one was going to come
faithfully through autumn
to the real river. I saw that.
No one was going to come.

Once the summer had its
light all around what is,
once time was deep enough,
nothing could suffice.

Belatedly I saw it:
in that valley for the great story,
unrolled, golden, waiting, open to the sun,
full of decision and leaves and shadow—

For me there was no one.

THAT AUTUMN INSTANT

You stand on a hill in July
and wave: you feel summer stream over
the land, part of a river too wide
to cross, ever—still and mild.
You feel that river turn on its back
and stare at the sky.

You turn to dive again for your life
where it leads you, by breath and
anything next. The daylight endures;
it won't pass; it follows the sun
around. But wherever you turn,
there on the grass and weeds
winter has brushed its hand.

THE INDIAN CAVE JERRY RAMSEY FOUND

Brown, brittle, wait-a-bit weeds
block the entrance. I untangle their
whole summer embrace. Inside—soot from
a cold fire, powder of bones,
a piece of ceremonial horn: cool
history comes off on my hands.
Outside, I stand in a canyon so
quiet its pool almost remembers its
old reflections. And then I breathe.

NORTH OF LIBERAL

You open your mouth to say, "Wait!"
then falter: far away,
the open, the winter, and
the four of you crunching snow
along the Cimarron.

That path is still there; it led
miles and miles into brown country
so far that to go there again
makes a new turn, almost makes
your life another person's.

You glance around. The world
has turned into now:
at a bluff on the north bank
forty years ago someone
did not come to meet you.

THE SUMMER GAME

All over the mountains we looked for
the best thing there is. The kids called
"Maybe this," "Maybe this." Every
time, they held a hand curved—
a shell, a rock, that kind of moss
that can unfold at zero. Or you
pointed and sighted over your hand.

And the sunlight crossed your palm like
never again. It was a day we
could put in the bank. No one
was mad at us; no one even knew
we were there. "Maybe this!" you said.

Yes.
Let's put the kids and the puppies
in the back of the pickup and go rummaging
over any old landscape again.

THE LITTLE ROOM

When I woke up at the beach
I saw my hand beside me
sleeping on a stone.
I remembered our room at home
like a wave inside a wave
that the ocean sends when it comes
through miles, through afternoons,
to slide close and enter the sand.

At a place like that, where we
have to know—that instant,
that clear space, that bright room
inside a wave—I wanted to stop,
not have to breathe. I wanted to wave
every sound back into the dream
and wait. There was a sky over
the sky. The years were all
back under your tongue. Nothing
we ever did was too late.

Then I moved my hand.

III

ANIMALS FULL OF LIGHT: POEMS 1970-1972

KINSHIP

In a wilderness at the end of a vine
it is now. Flowers are brushing toward noon.
From the dome of his skull in a room in
the earth, under the arch of the sky,
a caveman draws curves to link
hunter and prey. In that harness he put
on them all, the animals whine.

So even today, when we start to speak, then
turn away, I hear through contorted rock
a diagram rise through quiet—
that artist at work in the cave and a
tunneling heart—yours, mine—lost as
it ever was, racing to stay the same.

AT THE APOSTLE ISLANDS

We had a sled with a sail,
an island far over the ice,
and a whole day for the runners to cry
as they streaked the one
course left for them in the only
compromise our course would accept,
aimed always for home.

AQUARIUM AT SEASIDE

Groping stars called up from a field,
in silence curled these languid creatures,
abrupt as truth's edge, wander their schedule.
What great rope current braided us apart?
Into that night we follow those lives,
lonely like ours. With my tongue
I touch the glass: millions of years.
It divides the world.

FERNS

After the firestorms that end history,
a fern may print on the rock
some pattern about chance, and
the reaching for it, and the odds.

Already they are prints for us:
lace in the dusk, thin
stem, wide hand, faint presence; and
I know something fainter, fern:

The map under this country
that shows where we are while
we wander lost and the sun pulls
and our thought swims into the air.

A QUIET DAY AT THE BEACH

Gulls hit the silence and come through—
designs the wind offers to islands
that have no past or future but wind.

Down under the bridge the current is
talking. Pencils of sunlight are marking
this year along carefully faded boards.

A few of the minnows left over from
scenes before World War II explore what
might have happened if. . . .

In the slack tide I see a minnow so young
I can look through it and see the sand of
a world we are all beginning to love.

MR. FEAR

At the last he knew everyone.
Quiet at the edge of parties,
watching every face, he chose:
he usually took the fast cars home.

He always liked flags.

When he met the young, they
never forgot him, no matter
how quickly they turned away. And he
noted down their names.

At the shoulders of the old, he stared:
on them he laid his familiar hand.

He owned a vast collection of medals.

To those who said they did not
know him, he introduced himself.
Abruptly he gave them a startling smile.
They remembered that smile
long after they turned away.

THOSE LEAVES

Somewhere a forest, every
leaf still, far but clear.
Somewhere staggering pines
making it over a pass.

And somewhere a wind
ready to find far, lost men
and cover their tracks.
We walk on. Leaves blow past.

REMNANTS OF A POEM, OBSCURE PARTS BURNED AWAY IN A FREAK ACCIDENT AT THE OFFICE OF THE *WESTIGAN REVIEW*

Noon in the elms, wide noon,
and nobody left but the oriole
            thin long splinter of light
tree house fell

                        dark head that could not
save me   branch broke
body died.

Branch broke where the floor began
            tree house   world wanted tombstones
moved. That was August noon, that target
            fall. Under my lowered lids I go there.
Escape that day in the sun

                        body died.

SATURDAY NIGHTS

My hands reason with steel.
I charge into the room—turmoil; but
the order that might be dwells there,
calm as the ceiling, and I see it.
"Reach!" The crowd sees the two
dark eyes of the guns, unblinking.
If anything happens, the left
hand speaks first. The right,
in reserve, holds the veto.

The quiet I love descends.

Outside, my horse whistles.
The crowd yells, "Bill! Clowning
again!" We all belly up to the bar.
Inside it's warm, and my old horse
out there can just stamp all he wants
and whistle and creak in the wind.

Ending a visit,
going away, alone with a road and
meant for endings, I let the high beam
cut gray fields where morning is coming.
I rush for that step from clear into haze.
I leave the lights with the animals.

Back there somewhere, where your body stands,
a high energy finds you. I must
forget fast, leave you like a statue
shedding rain. I see you move
before there is time: air touches that stone
and our whole state begins two kinds of life—
the flash of encounter where light hits
and bunches your body, and this long day
down a country road going away,
a visit ended.

EARLY MORNING

Inside this dream to come awake,
be held above the ground, have air
catch me, then fall onward and know
it is a dream, then wake and be falling—

I love this dream, God, where
in a dream You have me dream
You, and come quiet into this place
and be Your waking.

SOME LIGHTS

You turn on a light in a room, and it
pours the silence all over your face.

All night by a campus path a light
shines under a reflector that spreads
rays out and down. Winter, summer,
deer from the deep woods turn their
extinguisher eyes, and above the path
leaves or branches make a long dome or corridor.
People go by. That glow in the woods—
it waits.

In a cave somewhere a passageway
goes down and a light falls dimmer and dimmer
but nobody goes there, and it is so still
that the stars above ground make a little tone
through the rocks, because—no matter how far—
you know those other lights have survived.
They are there.

TERMS OF SURRENDER

We hide in the dead grass.
Heat makes the rocks tremble.
Before night rescues us we have
accepted the terms: crawled,
lied, cheated—lived.

We take what the world gives.
We bow our heads like flowers
and think of the ways we came.
Before sleep each night we put
our mouths against a clod
and breathe our share of common air—

The truest way there is to say God's name.

AT ARCHBISHOP LAMY'S CHURCH
IN SANTA FE

A few leaves cling and skitter
along the walk. The wind pats
my jacket, my turned-up collar.

I have walked up the river, past
beer cans, by shops at the square. No one
in the town knew me or spoke.

Here in late winter light
remembering a clear, still life in the sun,
I touch a door with my shadow.

You down there in the stone, was it
easy when you knew the sun had other
places to go, and your part ended?

AT THE EDGE OF TOWN

Sometimes when clouds float
their shadows make dark fields,
wings that open. Just by looking
we become them. Is there a kingdom
where only the soundless have honor?
Some days, yes. We look up and follow.

WHERE WE LIVE

Inside a house I live, inside
a room that knowing makes, then
far inside something greater no one
can find or say.

And you live beside me,
millions of stars away.

A GLIMPSE BY THE PATH

"Mitten, follow that hand." All
day it did, at night holding
the shape that it had, easily, comforted.

I like such giving as that, the
grasping of what already is. You survive
that way, in this world,

This world that you accept with fear,
with no more to give:
you hold and are held, thrown away—

Glove in the snow, snow-filled.

CANADIAN

Hear the wild geese; know how their
eyes peer, feet fold into the down.
Open your eyes like that—see day
dawn at a certain height.

Hurt, cold, gleaming like
little stones high over the lakes,
the lakes in their heads pass, reading
the earth, finding the right wild place.

We can't be there; we can't
embrace what comes in a rush now,
now, while we hear the wild geese.

THE WAY IT WILL BE

Awake when the world turns over
you wait, hold your breath steady,
start the whole sky into the sky again
around a new day.

With your heart you could stop it—
not even breathe, make the birds
waiting for morning not wake.
It will happen. It has to. Some day.

A CHURCH KEEPS ON

No house can last, no house
holds like a mountain long, but
a church keeps on: the stone
that was interrupted continues
to be that stone, and the arch,
forsaken, leans wherever it's gone,
lost in its own story all the way down, still
whatever it was when we thought it strong.

THEN

Something will happen. You will hold
against the face of the days a still
mask, because you know.

Certain people will open the door.
They will stand awhile, glancing
miles away. At that moment you will last,

Sprung into the sky, forever like yesterday.

ANY JOURNEY

When God watches you walk, you are
neither straight nor crooked. The journey
stretches out, and all of its reasons
beat like a heart. Coming back, no triumph,
no regret, you fold into the curves,
left, right, and arrive. You touch
the door. The road straightens behind you.
It is now. It has all come true.

THE CONDITIONS

Torn when winter came,
leaves yet worshipped the sun.
But our time began when shadows fell,
after the sun was gone:

All those miles leading north,
hands out for any leaf,
through the cold nights, we walked
while only the river moved.

Long valley, no one, the wind
wild like a rough friend—
we never complained; it was good,
hearty, expected to end.

It did. We understood.

IT'S LIKE WYOMING

At sunset you have piled the empties and
come to the edge, where the wind kicks up
outside of town. A scatter of rain
rakes the desert. All this year's weather
whistles at once through the fence.

This land so wide, so gray, so still that
it carries you free—no one here need bother
except for their own breathing. You touch
a fencepost and the world steadies onward:
barbed wire, field, you, night.

TONIGHT

Tonight and another night linger
outside the door. One whispers to
the other and comes in alone. Where
will tomorrow be when that whispering
stops or the whisperer can't find
a friend to listen any more?

Out in the sky a comet will come
seeking the miles that promised
to be there. Then it will go on, cheated
but ready for any next plan.
Triggered by time and that vacant pass,
the world will circle in space alone—

Ever toward that other alone.

BEGINNING THE DAY

Waking
   It is still. No breeze, no one
   moving anywhere. In this town even the dogs
   are quiet. No car, train, plane.
   Nothing—Earth sailing
   through the sky forgotten.

Shaving and Getting Ready
   Someone is thinking of The Earth. I can
   feel the thought fumble past my face.
   When it comes back my shadow will touch
   that shadow. We will trade. My thought will
   find everything that ever brushed the world.

Crossing the Bridge to Work
   Children are digging along the river.
   They are looking for their names.
   One of them finds a shell, and suddenly
   I lean forward—that one is me! So fast
   he is, running away down the beach!
   I want to give him some other name.

MEDITATION

Animals full of light
walk through the forest
toward someone aiming a gun
loaded with darkness.

That's the world: God
holding still
letting it happen again,
and again and again.

IV

FINDING SMOKE'S WAY: POEMS 1973-1977

OUR LIFE

We should give it away, this breath,
and another, as easy as it came to us,
pray that it all be trust—
as it is, always, of course,
even when we gasp and fight:—
inhale what helps, exhale
those curses that hurt,
but always on solid earth,
so true, so near, so right.

WEST OF HERE

The road goes down. It stops at the sea.
The sea goes on. It stops at the sky.
The sky goes on.

At the end of the road—picnickers,
rocks. We stand and look out:

Another sky where this one ends?
And another sea?
And a world, and a road?

And what about you?
And what about me?

THE SAINT OF THOUGHT

One moment each noon, faced
where the sun is, turn
from events to the church in the stone.
The shade under your hand
welcomes you. Let the lamp
in your forehead explode.

In the long dive of your life
past the sun, these are important,
these meetings. Repeat:
"Rescue me, Day. Hills,
hold the light." Lift your hand.
Let the dark out.

A GIFT FOR KIT

Fence wire sang—spring wind—
where I stood among tumbleweeds, ready
to wander, too, by Willow Creek.

Listen—it was only the world
adrift in the days, and a sound
of the sky singing to it,

Where friends of mine once lived,
and I came there to understand: it was like
seeing, and knowing amid what you see.

A meadowlark brought me back,
just flying its road and singing,
being alive. I brought home this tumbleweed.

THINGS ABOUT THE SUN

Any time the sun
touches our part of the earth
we say the sun shines.

Sometimes dogs bark at the sun,
but I don't mind it.

There are flowers the sun never sees.

Many times I have said to it,
"Wait!" And it waited.

With the sun, it will be all right
after I'm gone.

Where it can, the sun endlessly
examines things, nothing too large
or small for long, long attention.
When I walk I would view
like that—all: rich, poor, young,
old, near, far. And I'd save a report
for whenever the sun does.

Mornings when it looks
at me, for an instant there are
all those other times.

SLANTS OF RAIN

Some of the rain past the searchlight
at the coast has found a forgotten
doll on the beach face down shuddering.
Restless to roving over the earth

I find a house on a hill.
I pass with a wish—happiness—
and I will leave them alone. But
what if they need me?

Where is the part of the earth
called "Go There, Go There"?

How hard it is to wander, for these stories!
—the other world so close,
the parables that do not get told.

We will go back, other years, but now
except for the slight turn when we feel
the wind veer, we are held.
There is no way.

Trees on the loyal mountain
march in their slow time.
They turn when I call.
They need me.

MANY THINGS ARE HIDDEN BY THE LIGHT

Now I remember, letting the dark
flood in, how we used to shoot animals,
and how they were afraid. We stared
into hedges. What we saw we killed.

Now I know by the cold: at night those hedges
run the crazy fields and we children of light
stagger and flash, lost where we triumph,
reeling our steadiness toward our terrible homes.

CAVE PAINTING

It was like the moon, the open before us,
when we came out of the last hills
we had to cross, to be tracked by the stars.
And whatever we said, we knew could be heard.
Then, we learned about caves, where you have
now discovered us, even these places. But
for awhile we painted our hidden lives
deep here, and we always tried—like
this I am doing now—to find ways
even deeper, with rooms that would
blaze only for us and those of our kind.
And even now—because a picture is a disguise—
you may never know our ultimate home with
Earth over it, and the silence where without
power or worth—with nothing—we first
learned to huddle together and foil the stars.

BY THE DESCHUTES SHORE

Millions of miles away at evening the sun
touches the little folded hands of the dead
mouse in the grass church by the river.
No tuft but gains a halo in the service, no
rock unwarmed. Having no hands, the world
learns everything by shouldering down in the
dusk and waiting like this while the sun
repeats its lesson color by color toward
the brown mouse, brown paws, brown, brown grass.

AT AN INTERVAL IN TALK

An owl call—round, globed as the moon—
floats from night through the open window
and brushes my face with the whole world
outside our home.

The woods flow back. The years I've had
have floated away. Without a sound
I turn my face and its hunger for the world,
here: today.

STILLNESS IS THE RIGHT WAVE

At the shore we always choose
one wave by time and place,
and call it best. When it
is over, choose another,
and at the last catch in a cup
a little one to pour on the sand.

Remember how?—it is like dreaming:
listen for the right wave; let
each one tell a story.
Never an end,
never an end.

Window means "wind eye," but
we forget at home. Some night a voice
catches up—"Where are we
going?" We remember how
dark among the stars,
how alone in a stall of space
the world is.

All that stillness comes
between the waves for us
outside the wind's eye.

ACROSS NEBRASKA

Popcorn spoke. A cathedral praised
then bowed behind. Hills voted
west, "Aye," "Aye," "Aye."
Trucks voiced inconsequences. In Hebron
the druggist's daughter looked a book
at us—her father hated motorcycles.
Oh City of Refuge, the land unreels and
popcorn speaks, "Rows, roads, horizons,
youth: Goodby, goodby, goodby."

GUTTERS OF JACKSON: CACHE STREET NORTH

Gum wrappers with nothing, Coors can
(flat), spilled—raspberry?—ice cream,
little torn flag, incredibly smashed pine
cone, Bud bottle half full of—maybe—
beer, gravel, gravel, piece of a
sign—"meet you at M...."—big
baked truck tread tracks in dried mud
climbing the curb, and across from the giant
timbers of the Chamber of Commerce, just where
town hesitates before the swooping scene,
one tiny shard of glass, blue, so
intense it shines like the Pharoah's eyes
in the dark when they closed his tomb.

FOR A MARKER

Where I lay first the grass
hummed, holding the wind.
Already earth,
coveting all I touched,
I suffered that sound—it was kind.

When I came to in the morning
all was a different sound—nighthawks at grass level
were working those air channels
their wide mouths found.

When you read this or hear it,
say a prayer for the owls:
they were the saddest I heard
that first long night I listened,
going into the ground.

HAPPY IN SUNLIGHT

Maybe it's out by Glass Butte some
time in late fall, and sage owns the whole
world. Even the obsidian chips
left by the Indians glitter, out of
their years. Last night's eager stars
are somewhere, back of the sky.

Nothing where you are says, "It's me
only." No matter how still the day,
a fence wire hums for whatever there is,
even if no one is there. And sometimes
for luck, by neglecting to succeed that day,
you're there, no one else, and the fence wire sings.

ANOTHER TWILIGHT

Sometime you will be in a shop,
some evening. The lights will come on
rippling forward, and the shelves
will wait, in their still way. Nights
empty as big dark windows
will line up for you.

Like that, I was here, and I stopped too.
Somewhere in stillness the lights
came on, winking their own pale being,
and I listened with all my life
for something else, quickly, the way you do.

CHARGED BY MOONLIGHT

Whatever this dance we're in, the moon
will come home some day—I will
see it on the kitchen floor, marking
the step to take—a silent silver
step, then a life as a new kind of being.

Deft, on the way to bed, I bow,
then go on, but better by that glimpse it seems,
carried into a dream, held
in a dance the world knows, caring
for me, a self like a frozen light.

ASSURANCE

You will never be alone, you hear so deep
a sound when autumn comes. Yellow
pulls across the hills and thrums,
or the silence after lightning before it says
its names—and then the clouds' wide-mouthed
apologies. You were aimed from birth:
you will never be alone. Rain
will come, a gutter filled, an Amazon,
long aisles—you never heard so deep a sound,
moss on rock, and years. You turn your head—
that's what the silence meant: *you're not alone*.
The whole wide world pours down.

THE WAY I DO IT

The best things we say, I
take them out and whisper them
into that hole in the pasture,
right down there where those
aspens have come up, trembling
all day—

And sometimes now when the air is right
I can hear those things breaking loose
from leaves and skittering away
downwind: everything slides through light
that is absolute, around and over and under
the leaves—

So I stand there and listen it back,
our talk: aspens lean their tongues
and lick the sun or the rain, and
with everything in the world to hope for
I start reaching far and calling out,
"Got it again!"—

Then I turn home and run and run.

LOOKING FOR YOU

Looking for you through the gray rain,
your whole house is a face, windows
for eyes, door for a mouth. Chimney
breathing, your house waits. You
come down the street: you get a stare,
straight and slow to change.

No matter how willing and weak your own
face is, you know another face
for you, somewhere in the world: your house,
or a stone you choose on a mountain, or even
the wrinkled sea and its friend the wind.

Far away on an island off Alaska
there's a village gone back to forest,
and there leaning and peering—totem poles,
gray cedar eyes, crest, beak:
all those faces at home, staring from shadows,

Looking for you through the gray rain.

SMOKE

Smoke's way's a good way—find,
or be rebuffed and gone:
a day and a day, the whole world home.

Smoke? Into the mountains I guess
a long time ago. Once here, yes,
everywhere. Say anything? No.

I saw Smoke, slow traveler, reluctant
but sure. Hesitant sometimes, yes,
because that's the way things are.

Smoke never doubts though:
some new move will appear.
Wherever you are, there is another door.

AN ALPHABETICAL LIST OF TITLES

Across Nebraska, 98

After Spring and Summer, 46

Another Twilight, 102

Any Journey, 78

Aquarium at Seaside, 59

Assurance, 104

At an Interval in Talk, 96

At Archbishop Lamy's Church in Santa Fe, 70

At Missoula, 36

Attenuate, 6

At the Apostle Islands, 58

At the Cabin, 14

At the Edge of Town, 71

Beaver People, 21

Before Anyone Died, 20

Beginning the Day, 82

Brother, 38

By the Deschutes Shore, 95

Canadian, 74

Cave Painting, 94

Charged by Moonlight, 103

A Church Keeps On, 76

The Conditions, 79

The Coyote in the Zoo, 44

The Day I Got the Good Idea, 26

The Design on the Oriole, 16

Discovery, 7

Early Morning, 67

Even Now, 25

A Farewell Picture, 32

Ferns, 60

For a Marker, 100

Fort Rock, 34

A Gift for Kit, 90

The Girl Who Died, Who Lived, 24

A Glimpse by the Path, 73

Gutters of Jackson: Cache Street North, 99

Happy in Sunlight, 101

The Indian Cave Jerry Ramsey Found, 51

Inland Murmur, 5

In Our State No One Ever, 48

In the Cold, 35

It Rode with Us, 27

It's Like Wyoming, 80

Just to Let You Know, 42

Kinship, 57

The Last Time, 12

A Letter Not Even to Deliver, 19

Light, and My Sudden Face, 30

The Little Room, 54

Looking for You, 106

Many Things Are Hidden by the Light, 93

Maybe Alone on My Bike, 29

Meditation, 83

Mr. Fear, 62

No One Who Trusts, 11

North of Liberal, 52

Not Policy, But Love, 10

On Her Slate at School, 31

Our Life, 87

Outreach, 9

Outside of Town, 47

Proportioning, 15

A Quiet Day at the Beach, 61

Rambling On, 66

Remembering a First-Grade Music Teacher, 45

Remnants of a Poem . . . , 64

R_X Creative Writing: Identity, 23

The Saint of Thought, 89

Saturday Nights, 65

Shells, 4

Slants of Rain, 92

Smoke, 107

Snapshot, 39

Some Lights, 68

Stillness Is the Right Wave, 97

Storm at the Coast, 40

Storm Warning, 3

The Stranger, 43

The Summer Game, 53

Survival, 37

Temporary Facts, 8

Terms of Surrender, 69

That Autumn Instant, 50

Then, 77

Things About the Sun, 91

Those Leaves, 63

Time Capsule, 33

Toad, 13

Tonight, 81

Tourist Country, 28

Viewing the Coast, 41

A Walk with My Father When I Was Eight, 22

The Way I Do It, 105

The Way It Will Be, 75

West of Here, 88

When We Got to Chitina, 49

Where We Live, 72

A NOTE ON THE AUTHOR

William Stafford was born in 1914, in Hutchinson, Kansas, and was educated at the University of Kansas and the University of Iowa, where he received his doctorate. His work has included stints as a laborer in sugar-beet fields, an oil refinery and the U.S. Forest Service. He has worked for the Church of the Brethren and for Church World Service, and taught in Kansas, Iowa, California, Indiana and Oregon, where he served for many years as Professor of English at Lewis and Clark College in Portland. He retired from teaching in 1980 and devotes much of his time to giving workshops and reading from his poetry throughout the U.S.

Mr. Stafford's poetry has been widely honored. He has received a National Book Award for poetry, a Guggenheim Fellowship and the Shelley Memorial Award. He served as Consultant in Poetry to the Library of Congress in 1970-71.